Mauzy's *Rare Depression Glass*

Barbara & Jim Mauzy

Schiffer Publishing Ltd

4880 Lower Valley Road, Atglen, Pennsylvania 19310

Dedication

For our favorite Paul nephew, Paul Schwartz. We've made many memories together fishing, hunting, swimming at Moose Inn Mind. We shared many experiences including the nonviolent take-over of Paul's Rock, the invasion of the Aquatic Cows, the final moments of Moxie's life. We know we've had some influence, and now that you're a collector we're not sure if our influence is positive or negative, but we look forward to making more memories with you.

Other Schiffer Glass Books by Barbara & Jim Mauzy

Mauzy's Depression Glass: A Photographic Reference and Price Guide. *5th Edition.* Size: 8 1/2" x 11" ■ 1000+ color photos ■ Price Guide/Index ■ 256 pp. ■ ISBN: 978-0-7643-2755-1 ■ hard cover ■ $29.95

Mauzy's Comprehensive Handbook of Depression Glass Prices. *8th Edition.* Size: 4" x 8 1/2" ■ 143 color photos ■ 224 pp. ■ISBN: 0-7643-2496-9 ■ soft cover ■ $9.95

Other Schiffer Glass Books on Barbara Mauzy

McKee Kitchen Glass of the Depression Years. Size: 8 1/2" x 11" ■ 327 color photos ■ Price Guide/Index ■ 144 pp. ■ISBN: 978-0-7643-3084-1 ■ soft cover ■ $29.99

Peanut Butter Glasses. *2nd Edition.* Barbara E. Mauzy. Size: 6" x 9" ■ 977 color photos ■ Value Guide ■ 128 pp. ■ ISBN: 0-7643-1477-7 ■ soft cover ■ $19.95

Copyright © 2008 by Barbara & Jim Mauzy
Library of Congress Control Number: 2008922920

Designed by "Sue"
Type set in Florens LPt/Zurich BT
ISBN: 978-0-7643-3031-5
Printed in China

Contents

Dear Readers,

It's been ten years and five editions of *Mauzy's Depression Glass.* This decade gave us lows and highs; we were blessed with three grandchildren and two new Westies, but we lost Jim's loving father and our wonderful Moxie. We've watched the Glass World go from "Mauzy who?" to "Barbara and Jim," and for that we are humbly grateful.

We've crisscrossed America with camera equipment in hand and have so appreciated the enthusiastic reception we've received from collectors and dealers offering their prized glassware for inclusion in our books. We've had the privilege of presenting some spectacular never-before-seen pieces in each and every edition. This book is a compilation of the most unusual, most spectacular, and most rare pieces of Depression Glass featured these past ten years.

We are hard a work on our next Depression Glass edition and invite you, our reader, to be a part of this ongoing project. If you can get an item or a collection to the Pennsylvania studio just let us know. We'd be honored to add your name to the listing in the front of our next book.

Barbara and Jim Mauzy
www.TPTT.net

Justification and Values

Careful consideration of each image presented in ten years of photographing glass, writing about pieces and patterns, and documenting little-known and unknown items and merits for inclusion in this book led us to create a three-part book. The glassware within this book is either a rare piece, a rare color, or shown with an unusual decoration such as metal additions or surface details.

Values are not considered or provided in this book, but rarity is. For example, we show a Bubble plate with gold embellishment, the only one we've seen so decorated thus far, and we show a pink Cameo pitcher that is perhaps the only one ever made. There is no way the Bubble pie plate has a value anywhere close to the Cameo pitcher, but both are unique and worthy of consideration and inclusion if this book is to be complete. Throughout all of our books we repeat this statement: Ultimately the value of any item is determined by the buyer and the seller.

The purpose of this book is to simply highlight the unique variations of glassware created by American glass manufacturers during the 1930s and 1940s.

Acknowledgments

Without the generous willingness of others to share their glassware and expertise our books would still be a dream. We appreciate every single person listed below as well as a few contributors who have opted to remain anonymous.

We can't emphasize enough that these collectors and dealers have been gracious enough to provide not only a piece of glass but a piece of themselves by sharing enthusiasm, information, and history, much of which has been woven through the pages of *Mauzy's Depression Glass*. These are the experts:

Susan Aguiar
Joanne Aldrich
Wendell J. Auck
Gene E. Bailey
Helen & Edward Betlow
John Bistoff
Jim Boorech
Jean & Wayne Boyd
Cindy Brown
Debbie & Randy Coe
Charles & Theresa Converse
Joyce & Jim Coverston, The Attic Annex
Mary Cooper
Tony DiBasilio
Charlie Diefenderfer
Diefenderfer's Collectibles & Antiques
Bill & Millie Downey
Vic Elliot & Diane Elliot
Corky & Becky Evans
Kyle & Barbara Ewing
Ken & Terri Farmer
Ruth Farrington
Margaret Farraher
Mark Fors, Marwig Glass Store

Patty & Bill Foti, Patty Ann's Depression & Elegant Glassware
Steve & Ann Franco
Gary Geiselman, Grandma's China Closet
Jewell Gowan
Patrick & Janet Hanrahan
Connie & Bill Hartzell
Rick Hirte, Sparkle Plenty Glassware
Lester Hockensmith
Frank Hooks
Fran & Tom Inglis
Helen Jones
Michael & Kathleen Jones
Debbie Knighten
Vic & Jean Laermans
Walt & Kim Lemiski, Waltz Time Antiques
Sandy Levine
Lynne & Jerry Mantione
Donna & Earl Martin
Kathy McCarney
Neil McCurdy, Hoosier Kubboard Glass
Fred McMorrow & Roger Daye

Rob Newbrough
Ken & Elaine Palmer
Melissa Paymen Pille & Brian Pille
Paul Reichwein
Dave Renner
Replacements, Ltd.
Julia & Jim Retzloff
Dale Riendeau
Michael Rothenberger, Mike's Collectibles
Darlene Schoppert
Cliff Schwartz
Staci & Jeff Shuck, Gray Goose Antiques
Faye & Robert Smith
John Spack
Jeanne A. Spaid
Jesse Speicher
Ian Warner & Mike Posgay
Marie Talone
Raymond & Shirley Wagoner
Kevin L. Weiss
Patrick R. Williams
Lois Wrightman & Roger Hayman

1

Rare Pieces of Depression Glass

Glassware featured in this chapter is rare and therefore difficult to find. Some of the pieces are thought to be the only one known to exist, others are simply few and far between. Pieces in this chapter are often the highest priced items in Mauzy values listings or shown as too rare to price. Finding one of these pieces may be more difficult than affording it, but sometimes simply being in the right place at the right time can provide a thrilling opportunity to add a treasure to one's collection for a minimal investment.

Parrot (Sylvan) pitcher. *Courtesy of John Spack.*

Adam lamp shown in green; it is also found in pink. *Courtesy of Melissa Payne Pille and Brian Pille.*

American Sweetheart 6.5" diameter, 2" deep console bowl. *Courtesy of Margaret Farraher.*

Beaded Block 4.25" tall syrup pitcher with attached base designed to catch drippings. *Courtesy of Neil McCurdy, Hoosier Kubboard Glass.*

Bubble ruffled whimsy, perhaps the only one made. *Courtesy of Debbie and Randy Coe.*

Pink Cameo pitcher, thought to be the only one made.

Cameo sandwich server with center handle.

Cherry Blossom covered casserole, thought to be the only one made. *Courtesy of Ken and Elaine Palmer.*

Cherry Blossom 3.25" tall salt and pepper shakers. Less than a dozen vintage shaker sets exist. *Courtesy of Raymond and Shirley Wagoner.*

Cherry Blossom cookie jar, thought to be the only one. *Courtesy of Raymond and Shirley Wagoner.*

Cherry Blossom ruffled bowls made from the 7″ salad plate and the 6″ sherbet plate. These whimsies may be one-of-a-kind. *Courtesy of Raymond and Shirley Wagoner.*

Cherry Blossom 9″ x 5.25″ platter. *Courtesy of Raymond and Shirley Wagoner.*

Cherry Blossom 2.25" deep ruffled violet bowl made by crimp-
ing a saucer. *Courtesy of Raymond and Shirley Wagoner.*

Cherry Blossom 5-part divided relish tray. *Courtesy of Raymond and Shirley Wagoner.*

Cherry Blossom 9" rimmed plate with stippling. Two of these plates are known to exist. *Courtesy of Raymond and Shirley Wagoner.*

Cherry Blossom 10.25" diameter rimmed dinner plate. *Courtesy of Raymond and Shirley Wagoner.*

Cherry Blossom 8" diameter plate with twelve sides.
Courtesy of Raymond and Shirley Wagoner.

Cherry Blossom 8.5" diameter plate with twelve
sides. *Courtesy of Raymond and Shirley Wagoner.*

Cherry Blossom 2.75". 5.75" diameter comport made from a footed tumbler. Note the starburst motif on the foot, a design element not usually seen on this pattern. *Courtesy of Raymond and Shirley Wagoner.*

Cherry Blossom 6.5" tall pitcher with panels. The Cherry Blossom motif is only at the top. *Courtesy of Grandma's China Closet.*

Chinex Classic lamp. *Courtesy of Steve and Ann Franco.*

Coronation stemmed sherbet and pitcher. When we first photographed the sherbet we had no idea how rare this seemingly common piece is, but we haven't seen one since. The same is true for the pitcher, but one would have presumed the sherbet to be easily found. *Courtesy of Kyle and Barbara Ewing.*

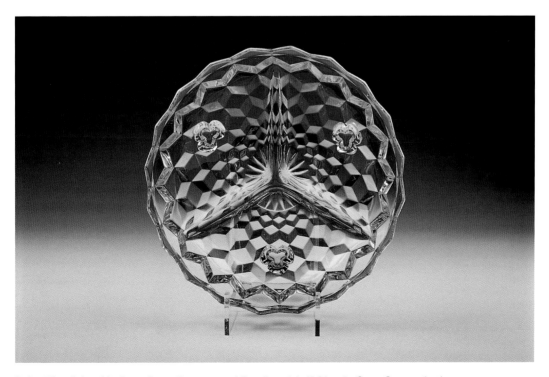

Cube 7" relish with three feet. *Courtesy of Staci and Jeff Shuck, Gray Goose Antiques.*

Cupid samovar (missing spout).

English Hobnail jade-ite sherbet, 2.25" tall, 4.5" diameter. *Courtesy of Ruth Farrington.*

English Hobnail jade-ite three-ounce cocktail with a square foot and eleven-ounce iced tea tumbler. *Courtesy of Sandy Levine.*

Fire-King Restaurantware 10.25" plate in jade-ite. The only other 10.25" plate known to exist is in the Anchor Hocking Morgue. *Courtesy of Jim Boorech.*

Fire-King Sapphire Blue Ovenware, Binky's Nip Cap nipple cover.

Fire-King Swirl dinnerware in Rose-ite, a pink opaque glass. Shown are the sherbet, berry bowl, and sugar bowl; any pieces of Rose-ite are rare. *Courtesy of Jesse Speicher.*

Floragold 9.5" diameter, 2.25" deep ruffled bowl made with a variation of the "normal" motif. *Courtesy of Mary Cooper.*

Floragold 7.75" diameter, 4" deep three-footed bowl. *Courtesy of Bill and Millie Downey.*

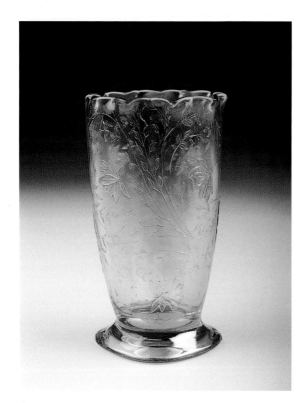

Floragold vase or celery.
Courtesy of Paul Reichwein.

Floral 6.75″ eight-sided vases. *Courtesy of Diefenderfer's Collectibles and Antiques.*

Floral 11″ faceted rim platter.

Floral 9" diameter, 2.75" tall comport. *Courtesy of Dale Riendeau.*

Florentine 2 paneled pitchers and tumblers. The pitchers are 7" tall and the tumblers are 4.25" tall and 3.25" in diameter. *Courtesy of Darlene Schoppert.*

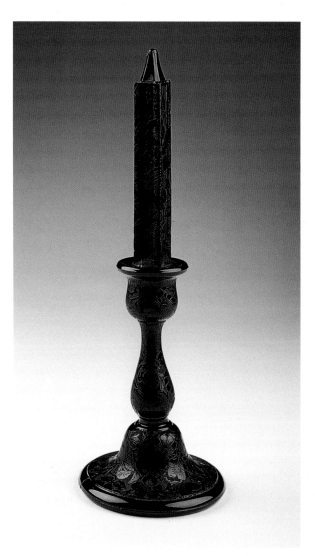

Flower Garden with Butterflies candlestick and candle. *Courtesy of Neil McCurdy, Hoosier Kubboard Glass.*

Forest Green compote, 6" diameter, 5.5" tall. This resembles a giant sherbet.

Fruits 7.5" diameter whimsy thought to be one of two known to exist. *Courtesy of Helen Jones.*

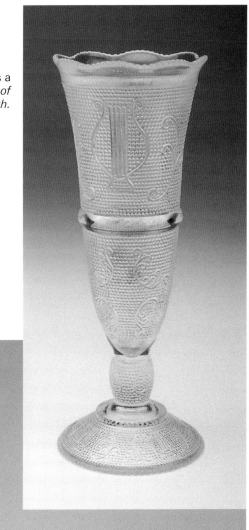

Harp vase in a variation that includes a ball of glass above the foot. *Courtesy of Lester Hockensmith.*

Iris chandelier. *Courtesy of Faye and Robert Smith.*

Iris flower bowl, an 11.5" ruffled bowl with a glass flower frog.

Iris whimsy made from 6" cereal bowl. *Courtesy of Fran and Tom Inglis.*

Iris cake plate lid. Several are known to exist. *Courtesy of Wendell J. Auck.*

Jubilee cut on Lancaster Glass Company blank. *Courtesy of John Bistoff.*

Madrid Lazy Susan. *Courtesy of Charles and Theresa Converse.*

Madrid gravy boat on tray/under platter. *Courtesy of Corky and Becky Evans.*

Mayfair lamp made using the candy jar. *Courtesy of Faye and Robert Smith.*

Mayfair sugar bowl with lid. The sugar bowl is common but there are only ten pink sugar lids known to exist and several of these are damaged. *Courtesy of Vic and Jean Laermans.*

Rock Crystal Flower 11.5" diameter five-part relish in milk glass. The underside is pictured as this shows the Rock Crystal Flower design. *Courtesy of Michael Rothenberger, Mike's Collectibles.*

Rosemary transitional tumbler which merges Federal Glass Company's Mayfair pattern with their Rosemary pattern. *Courtesy of Connie and Bill Hartzell.*

Royal Lace 5.5" diameter, 2.25" deep nut bowls. *Courtesy of Patrick R. Williams.*

Royal Lace 68-ounce pitcher in green. Rarely seen anywhere, several are known to exist in Canada. *Courtesy of Fran and Tom Inglis.*

Royal Lace 11" diameter, 3" deep rolled and ruffled bowl, thought to be the only one made. *Courtesy of Jeanne A. Spaid, 80 West Antiques.*

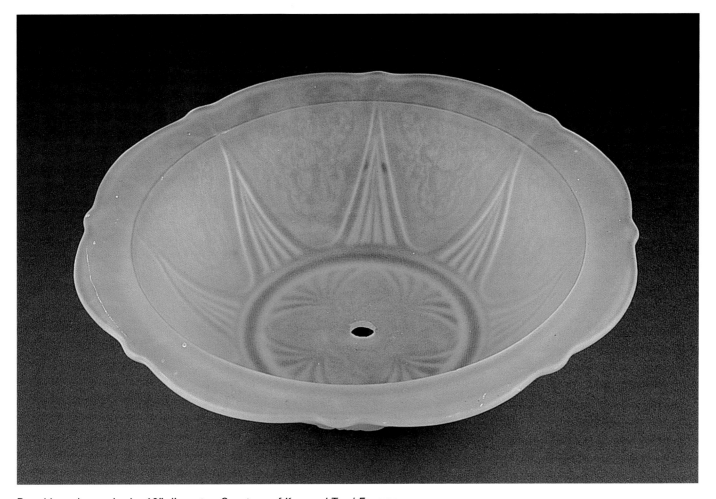

Royal Lace lamp shade, 10" diameter. *Courtesy of Ken and Terri Farmer.*

Sunflower 8" plate. Not only is this a unique size, the Sunflower design is slightly different from the "normal" dinner plate. *Courtesy of Replacements, Ltd.*

Sandwich (Indiana Glass Company) creamer with an unusual shape. The handle is pulled to the point of being too small for a finger to be inserted. *Courtesy of Faye and Robert Smith.*

Sunflower hot plate or trivet.

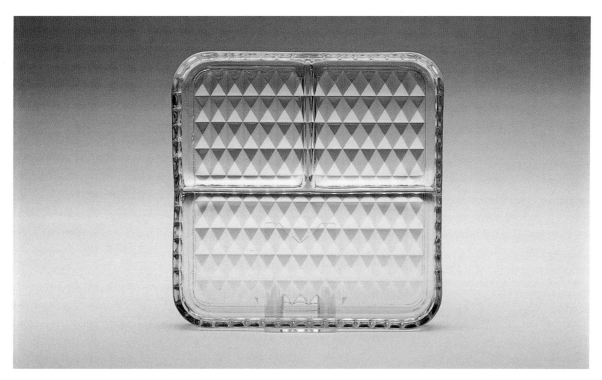

Windsor 8.25" square three-part relish. *Courtesy of Walt and Kim Lemiski, Waltz Time Antiques.*

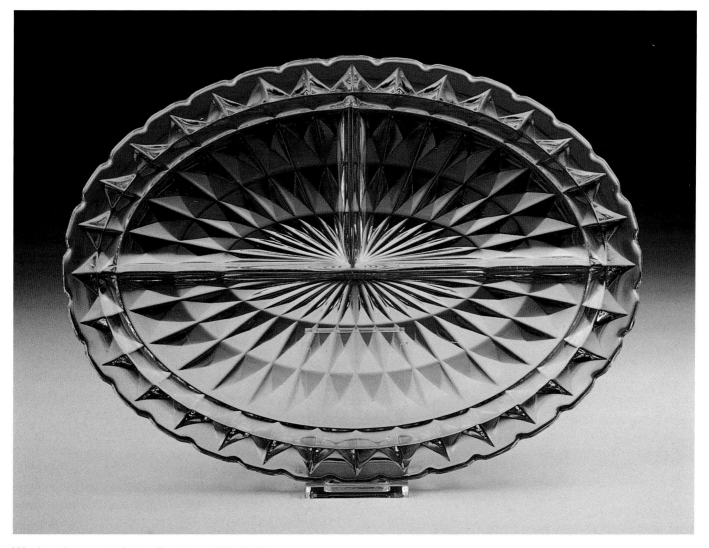

Windsor three-part platter. *Courtesy of Marie Talone.*

2

Unusual Color Variations of Depression Glass

This chapter focuses on known pieces of Depression Glass, some quite common, that have been created with a bit of panache. Chapter Two glassware presents colors not normally associated with the particular pattern in which it was made; some pieces have more than one color, some pieces are flashed with iridescence or another hue, some pieces are decorated with silver overlaid, and so on.

A truly committed collector seeks to own everything and anything in the pattern of choice and would probably be thrilled to find one of these unique pieces. Dealers who strive to have the outrageous, rare, and different will also experience the excitement of discovering something uncommon. The fun thing about these pieces is often they are not recognized by the novice dealer as something special and therefore they are regularly undervalued. For those of you of the hunting and gathering ilk, you may be rewarded for diligent searching with the discovery of another variation not shown here, and chances are you will do so with relatively little investment. The lesson here: never stop hunting for treasures!

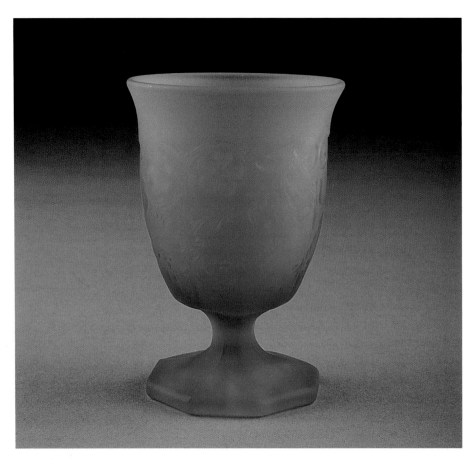

Rock Crystal Flower 3.75" tall, 2.5" diameter blue frosted or satinized stem. *Courtesy of Joanne Aldrich.*

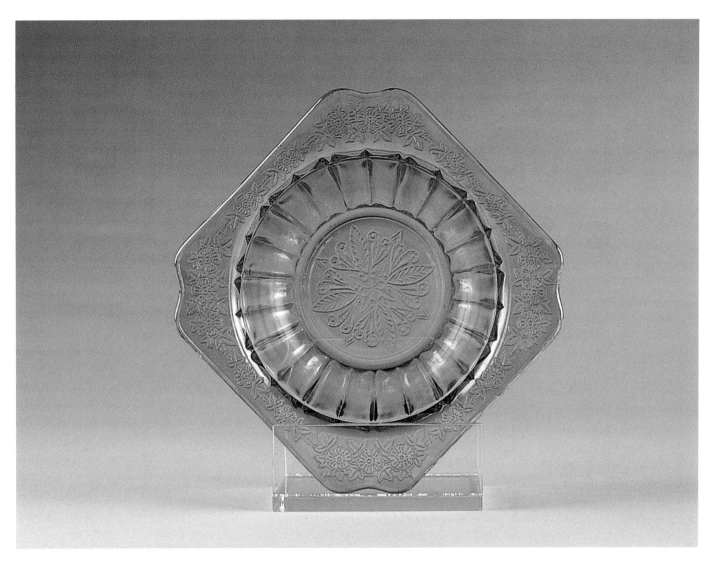

Adam iridized pink 4.75" berry bowl. This coloration is uncommon in any pattern.
Courtesy of Jean and Wayne Boyd.

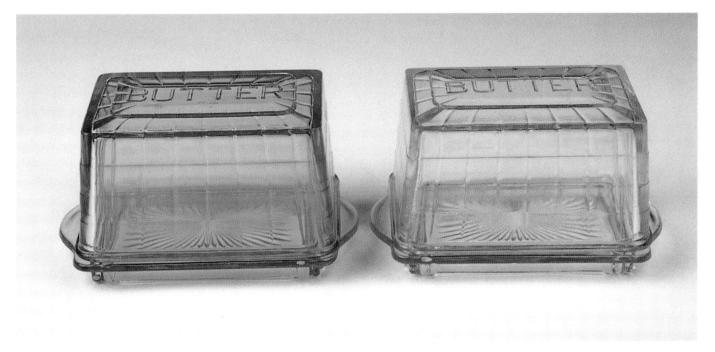

Block Optic rectangular one pound butter dishes. Common in green, both crystal (clear) and ice blue are hard, if not impossible, to find. *Courtesy of Patrick and Janet Hanrahan.*

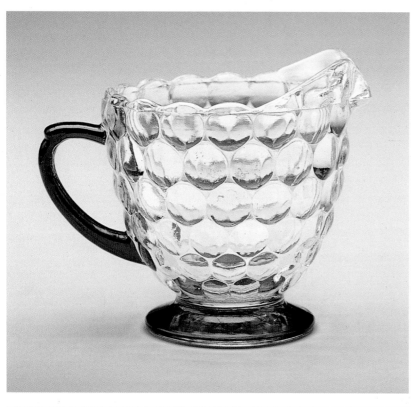

Bubble creamer with a handled and foot decorated with ruby flash. A matching sugar was made. *Courtesy of Walt and Kim Lemiski, Waltz Time Antiques.*

Bubble 6.75" bread and butter plate and cup in teal/ice blue. It is still unknown what else was made in this color-pattern combination. *Courtesy of Ian Warner and Mike Posgay.*

Bubble 7.75" diameter and 7" diameter light green bowls. It is still unknown what else was made in this color-pattern combination but based on what is shown here perhaps there is a great deal more to be documented. *Courtesy of Gene E. Bailey.*

Bubble light green 6.75" plate and saucer. *Courtesy of Donna and Earl Martin.*

Cherry Blossom 10.25" diameter, 3.25" deep bowl with three feet in orange slag with yellow-green trim. *Courtesy of Raymond and Shirley Wagoner.*

Cherry Blossom 8.75" diameter (11" handle to handle), 2.75"-3" deep bowl in orange slag with yellow-green trim. This may be one-of-a-kind. *Courtesy of Raymond and Shirley Wagoner.*

Cherry Blossom almost 9" diameter (10.75" handle to handle), bowl in Amberina.
This may be one-of-a-kind. *Courtesy of Raymond and Shirley Wagoner.*

Cherry Blossom 8.5" diameter, 2.5" deep yellow berry bowl. *Courtesy of Raymond and Shirley Wagoner.*

Cherry Blossom 4.5" tall, 3" diameter footed tumblers. Left, iridescent; right, reddish hue. Note: this pattern is being reproduced in ruby, but this tumbler is authentic. *Courtesy of Raymond and Shirley Wagoner.*

Cherry Blossom 10.75" diameter, (12.75" diameter handle to handle) 2.75"-3" deep tray with two handles. *Courtesy of Raymond and Shirley Wagoner.*

Cherry Blossom 9" yellow dinner plate.
Courtesy of Raymond and Shirley Wagoner.

Cherry Blossom 4.25" tall, nine-ounce crystal (clear) tumbler. Crystal Cherry Blossom is difficult to find, and it is not known which pieces were made in this color. *Courtesy of Raymond and Shirley Wagoner.*

Cherry Blossom 4.75" diameter, 1.5" deep and 8.5" diameter, 2.75" deep bowls with frosted sections. *Courtesy of Raymond and Shirley Wagoner.*

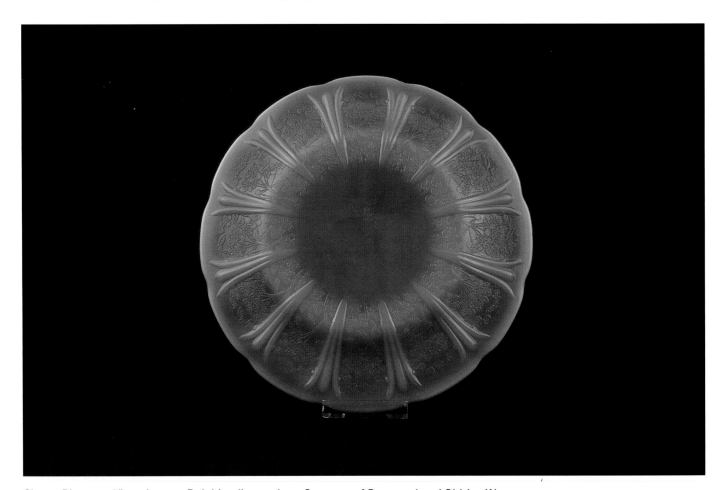

Cherry Blossom 9" opalescent Delphite dinner plate. *Courtesy of Raymond and Shirley Wagoner.*

Cherry Blossom jade-ite saucers. Note that the motif is on the underside. *Courtesy of Rob Newbrough.*

Cherry Blossom jade-ite 10.5" diameter two-handled sandwich tray. Note that the motif is on the underside. *Courtesy of Raymond and Shirley Wagoner.*

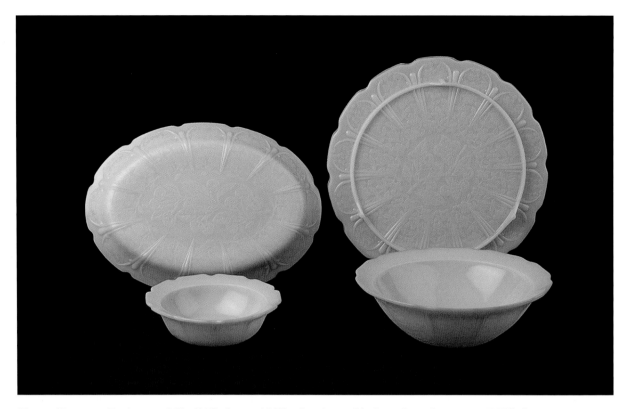

Cherry Blossom. Back row: 11" x 7.5" platter, 10.5" cake plate with three feet; front row: 5.75" diameter, almost 1.75" deep cereal bowl; 8.5" diameter, 2.5" deep berry bowl. *Courtesy of Rob Newbrough.*

Cherry Blossom jade-ite 9" grill plate. Note that the motif is on the underside.
Courtesy of Raymond and Shirley Wagoner.

Colonial, "Knife & Fork" 4" tall, 3" diameter tumbler.
Courtesy of Faye L. Smith.

Colonial, "Knife & Fork" 4" tall, 2.25" diameter iridescent and clear goblet. *Courtesy of Gene E. Bailey.*

Della Robbia Lavender Mist. 9" luncheon plate without a center design, 14" torte plate, 9" luncheon plate. This pattern was produced in a vast array of colors, but this hue is rarely found. *Courtesy of Tony DiBasilio.*

English Hobnail pieces with blue fired-on bases. 15.5" tall candy jar, two 5.5" tall candlesticks, 8.75" diameter, 6" deep bowl with a lid. We have seen two of these sets. *Courtesy of Fred McMorrow and Roger Daye.*

English Hobnail master candy jar in fired-on red with a gold foot. *Courtesy of Michael Rothenberger, Mike's Collectibles.*

Floral 4.75" tall footed tumbler, thought to be the only one made. *Courtesy of Vic Elliot and Diane Elliot.*

Floral bowl and plate in pumpkin orange. *Courtesy of Charlie Diefenderfer.*

Floral Delphite 4" diameter berry bowl. *Courtesy of Helen and Edward Betlow.*

Floral plate in tortoise shell, thought to be the only one
made. *Courtesy of Charlie Diefenderfer.*

Floral creamer and sugar bowl. *Courtesy of Vic and Jean Laermans.*

Floral Delphite 11″ faceted rim platter. *Courtesy of Charlie Diefenderfer.*

Florentine One footed tumbler. This is crystal (clear) glass that was cast in copper, thought to be the only one made. We have seen no other Depression Glass with this treatment. *Courtesy of Mark Fors, Marwig Glass Store.*

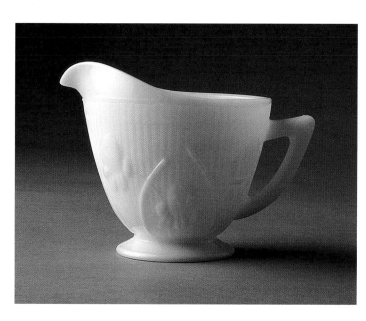

Iris creamer in milk white glass. Vintage Iris creamers and sugars made in a variety of transparent pastel colors were distributed in the United Kingdom.

Iris with ruby flash. Demitasse cup, candy jar with lid, 4.25" tall wine goblet. *Courtesy of Diane Elliot and Victor Elliot.*

Iris with ruby flash and hand painted flowers. Unfortunately ruby flash found on this pattern is often compromised. Back: 11.5" fruit bowl, front: 11.5" bowl with foot, 11.5" nut bowl. *Courtesy of Diane Elliot and Victor Elliot.*

Iris ruby flash candlesticks and 11.75" diameter sandwich plate in silver overlaid. *Courtesy of Diane Elliot and Victor Elliot.*

Iris with ruby flash trim. 4" stemmed sherbet, 11.75" diameter sandwich plate, 6" footed tumbler. *Courtesy of Diane Elliot and Victor Elliot.*

Lace Edge satin-finished cookie jar and lid with gold embellishment.

Miss America jade-ite 4.5" tall water tumbler. *Courtesy of Charlie Diefenderfer.*

Miss America 8.75"straight-sided bowl in smoked iridescence, thought to be the only one made. *Courtesy of Charlie Diefenderfer.*

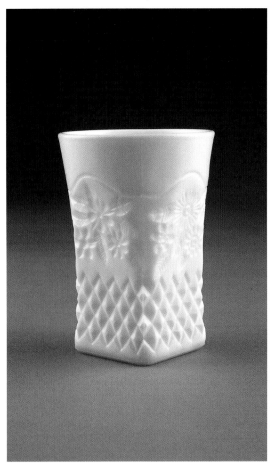

Pineapple and Floral milk glass 4" tall, 3" diameter tumbler. Although this is a pattern in low demand, it is worth noting that even this unimportant pattern has oddities to be recognized. *Courtesy of Gene E. Bailey.*

Pretzel 6.25" plate with tab in fired-on blue. This is a pattern normally thought of with crystal (clear) pieces. The coloration is on top of crystal glass. *Courtesy of Walt and Kim Lemiski, Waltz Time Antiques.*

Pretzel 8.25" salad plate in fired-on pink. This is a pattern normally thought of with crystal (clear) pieces. The coloration is on top of crystal glass. *Courtesy of Walt and Kim Lemiski, Waltz Time Antiques.*

Ring 5" tall, 2.75" tumbler. This is a pattern most commonly found in crystal (clear) with decorative stripes in various colors. Transparent green and transparent pink is less often seen, and red Ring is quite elusive. *Courtesy of Michael Rothenberger, Mike's Collectibles.*

Ring 5.5" deep, 5" diameter ice bucket in a less common color pattern. *Courtesy of Grandma's China Closet.*

Rock Crystal Flower is a pattern with a plethora of colors. Shown are 8.5" tall candle-sticks in teal and frosted/satinized yellow. *Courtesy of Joanne Aldrich.*

Rock Crystal Flower 8.5" diameter, 3.75" tall comport in satinized yellow. Are there other pieces of Rock Crystal Flower in this color? *Courtesy of Michael Rothenberger, Mike's Collectibles.*

Rock Crystal Flower in orange slag. This bowl is 12" in diameter and almost 6" deep. *Courtesy of Joanne Aldrich.*

Rock Crystal Flower 10.25" diameter, 3.5" deep scalloped bowl in a rarely-seen shade of blue. *Courtesy of Rick Hirte, Sparkle Plenty Glassware.*

Rock Crystal Flower 10.25" diameter, 3.5" deep bowl in Vaseline. *Courtesy of Jewell Gowan.*

Royal Lace in amethyst. 11" diameter, 3.5" deep rolled edge console
bowl and matching 5.25" diameter, 1.75" rolled edge candleholders.
Courtesy of Patrick R. Williams.

Royal Lace golden yellow 5.25" diameter, 1.75" rolled edge candleholder.
Courtesy of Jean and Wayne Boyd.

Sandwich (Anchor Hocking) 3.5" tall, 2.25" diameter tumbler.
Courtesy of Gene A. Bailey.

Sharon iridescent cup. It is unknown if other pieces of Sharon were iridized. *Courtesy of Gene A. Bailey.*

Spiral Optic (Jeannette Glass Company) 3.5" tall iridescent sherbet with a crystal foot. *Courtesy of Julia and Jim Retzloff.*

Spiral Optic (U.S. Glass Company) fired-on 8.5" tall candlestick. These colors were applied to crystal (clear) glass. *Courtesy of Julia and Jim Retzloff.*

Sunflower creamer and sugar. This is a pattern normally found in transparent pink and transparent green. *Courtesy of Staci and Jeff Shuck, Gray Goose Antiques.*

Twisted Optic (Imperial Glass Company) iridized glassware. 9.25" diameter, 2.25" deep rolled edge console bowl, 8.25" tall candle holder with a clear base. *Courtesy of Julia and Jim Retzloff.*

Waterford 12″ diameter tray in frosted yellow. It is not known if other frosted yellow pieces were made.
Courtesy of Patty & Bill Foti, Patty Ann's Depression & Elegant Glassware.

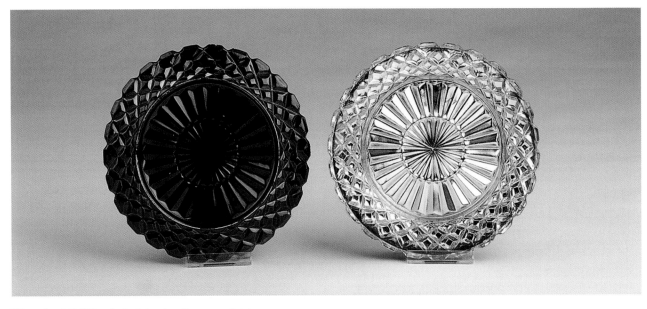

Waterford 7.25″ salad plates in silver overlaid.

Windsor with ruby flash. 7.25" bowl with three feet, candlesticks, smooth-rim sugar with pointy-knobbed lid, and creamer. *Courtesy of Cindy Brown, Susan Aguiar, and Debbie Knighten.*

Windsor 8.25" diameter, 2.5" deep bowl in Amberina. *Courtesy of Joanne Aldrich.*

3

Unique Decorations on Depression Glass

Ormolu, gold, silver. These are all details added to Depression Glass, often after the glass left the factory. Undecorated American glass sent to Canada was exempt from certain tariffs if ornamentation was added by the hands of Canadian artisans. For this reason, many of the items featured in Chapter Three were generously shared by Canadian collectors or found in Canada. Such is the case of the spectacular Victory bowl featured here.

American entrepreneurs also contributed to the creative enhancement of Depression Glass. Manufacturers of metal products would purchase bulk quantities of glassware, add their own touches, and then offer the new and improved glassware to the retailer. In some cases an individual with metal or glass cutting skills would purchase glass, embellish it, and then market it. These home-grown businessmen sometimes functioned in an environment as utilitarian as a garage with one simply goal: bring money into the home during an era of extreme poverty and suffering.

In some instances additional embellishments enhance the value of the piece, but the extra details may diminish collectors' interest. As an example consider the Manhattan pattern. Few collectors seek the satinized glassware found with metal handles, trim, and other ormolu, thus these items are valued less than the plain counterparts. However, the Manhattan ashtray with the beer advertisement is much more rare than originally thought when photographed in 1998; no others have been seen since and many have contacted us in an attempt to acquire one. Value is a direct function of supply and demand. Even an item in low in supply will have a suppressed value if there is little demand for ownership.

Also featured are several interesting pieces of metalware obviously made to enhance or accompany specific pieces of Depression Glass.

Glassware in this chapter is unique; it is worthy of one's attention acknowledging that not all items are of great value. In many ways this chapter is the most fun!

Victory 12" diameter, 2.25" deep console bowl with unusual embellishment on the rim.

American Sweetheart 11"
metal tray. *Courtesy of Vic
and Jean Laermans.*

American Sweetheart din-
ner plate, cup, and saucer
trimmed in gold. The din-
ner plate has a rose motif
painted in the center and
is signed "EZ." *Courtesy
of Kathy McCarney.*

American Sweetheart 10.25" dinner plate with "TOWER OF EMPIRE SOUVENIR EMPIRE EXHIBITION - SCOTLAND - 1938." *Courtesy of Ken and Terri Farmer.*

Anniversary bowls (7.25" soup and 4.75" berry) have been elevated to new heights. *Courtesy of Cliff Schwartz.*

Bubble 8.25″ vegetable bowl in regal glamour. *Courtesy of Cliff Schwartz.*

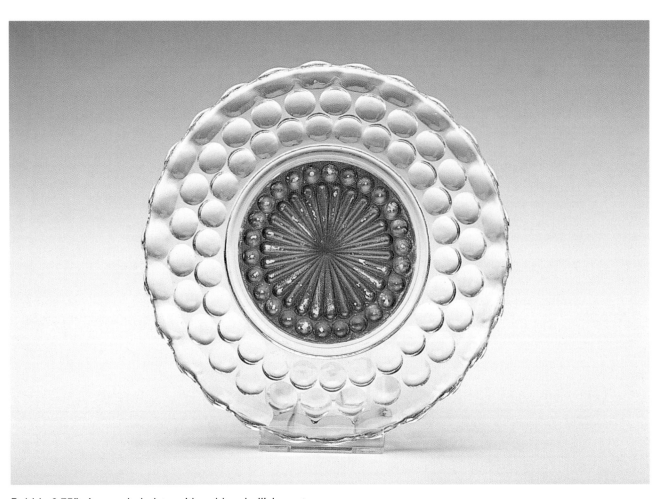

Bubble 6.75" pie or salad plate with gold embellishment.

Bubble 5.25" cereal bowl in hammered aluminum rim.

Crow's Foot 6.5" diameter candy dishes with sterling silver decorations. Left: 25th anniversary; right: floral motif. *Courtesy of Michael Rothenberger, Mike's Collectibles.*

Doric three-part candy dishes would fit in the 8.5" hammered aluminum tray manufactured by Everlast. *Courtesy of Kevin L. Weiss.*

Forest Green ashtrays on top and on bottom. *Courtesy of Frankie Hooks.*

Iris 8" beaded rim berry bowl advertising Babcock Furniture. *Courtesy of Walt Lemiski and Kim Lemiski.*

Iris with gold trim: sugar base and lid and 11.75" sandwich plate. *Courtesy of Diane Elliot and Victor Elliot.*

Manhattan and Queen Mary with metal embellishments, additions made after the factory. Manhattan 8" vase, Queen Mary satinized 4" candlesticks, Manhattan 9.5" diameter fruit bowl. *Courtesy of Walt Lemiski and Kim Lemiski.*

Manhattan ashtray with advertisement, the only one we've ever seen. *Courtesy of Michael and Kathleen Jones.*

Manhattan 4.5" sauce bowl with handles, satinized and embellished.
Courtesy of Michael Rothenberger, Mike's Collectibles.

Moderntone sugar with metal lid. This is a perfect example of a metal manufacturer adding a detail to glassware. There is no glass lid for the sugar bowl, and there are other metal lid designs, but this is the hardest-to-find lid that is aesthetically appropriate. *Courtesy of Charlie Diefenderfer.*

Moderntone Platonite dinnerware with monograms. Glass company executives would commission wares for gifts and to use on special occasions. There is no history on these pieces, but it is likely they were produced for a specific purpose in limited quantities. Back row: sherbet, 8.75" dinner plate, 6.75" salad plate; front row: 5" berry bowl, 5.75" sherbet plate, sugar.

Moderntone Platonite dinnerware decorated to be a Bridge Set. It is likely that this was made at the factory, albeit in very limited supplies as we have not seen this set or pieces of this set since selling this in 1999. Card parties were a regular part of American socializing and glass manufactures created all sorts of accessories to meet the needs of the hostess. This set consists of one 10.5" sandwich plate, four 7.75" luncheon plates, four cups, four saucers, one creamer, and one sugar.

Old Café 8" low and flared mint tray with two embellishments: gold overlay on the underside of crystal (clear) glass and a detachable metal handle.

Petalware 8" salad plate with orange stripes. There are many striped arrangements to be found decorating Petalware, but this is the one and only plate we've found with orange details.

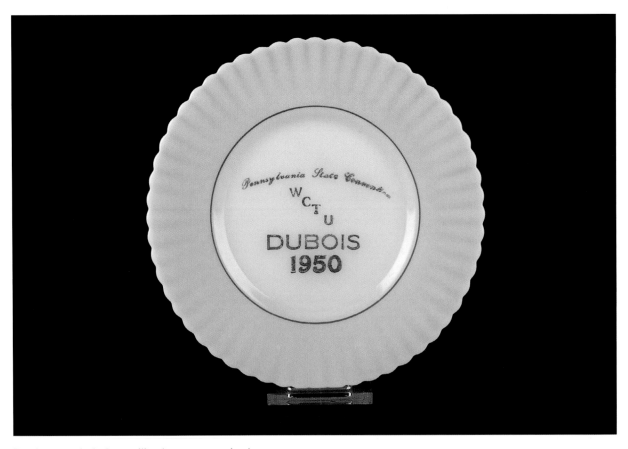

Petalware salad plate utilized as a souvenir plate.

Radiance 10" tall pitcher with sterling silver overlay. *Courtesy of Joyce and Jim Coverston, The Attic Annex.*

Ring Tumbler with chrome stem and foot.

Royal Lace sherbets on chrome bases with 6.5" diameter chrome indented plates clearly made to be used with the sherbets. *Courtesy of Fran and Tom Inglis.*

Juice tumblers with gold overlays. *Courtesy of Fran and Tom Inglis.*

Royal Lace straight edge candle holders with ruby rims. It is not known if other crystal (clear) Royal Lace is so decorated. *Courtesy of Patrick R. Williams.*

Sierra 5.5" cereal bowl in a sterling silver bowl that was obviously made to fit this specific item. *Courtesy of Walt and Kim Lemiski.*

Spiral (Hocking Glass Company) 9.5″ sandwich server with gold
trim and decorations. *Courtesy of Julia and Jim Retzloff.*

Sunburst 8" x 5.5" two-part relish with sterling silver overlay. *Courtesy of Fran and Tom Inglis.*

Tea Room 8.5" bowl with two handles with hand painted embellishment. Hand painted details are not uncommon on Depression Glass, but this pattern was produced primarily for commercial applications in restaurants, and this delicate addition would be incompatible with the intended use of the glassware. *Courtesy of Charlie Diefenderfer.*

Waterford 4" diameter ashtray with Post Cereal advertisement. One can assume this was free with the purchase of Post products. *Courtesy of Lois Wightman and Roger Hayman.*

Waterford 8.25" diameter, 3" deep berry bowl with chrome embellishments. *Courtesy of Lois Wightman and Roger Hayman.*

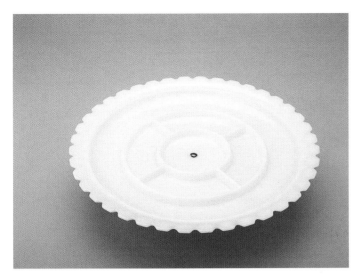
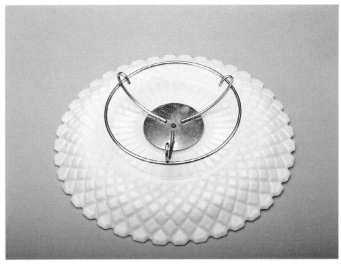

Waterford 14″ diameter six-part relish with metal base creating a Lazy Susan.

Waterford 13.75″ Lazy Susan with aluminum and Lucite additions.

Index by Pattern Name

Index by
Mauzy's Depression Glass Edition